AF322687

I've Always Loved You
An IVF Story
Written by:
Suzanne Castner
Illustrated by:
Anastasia Khmelevska

For my IVF babies
Ella and Charlotte

Our biggest wish was you.
Our daughter, or our son.
To grow our family
with you, my little one.

Heartbreak and defeat -
just no end, it seemed.
We called on expert help
to reach all we had dreamed.

It was time for IVF,
and many shots to do.
Two small parts were joined,
the building blocks of you.

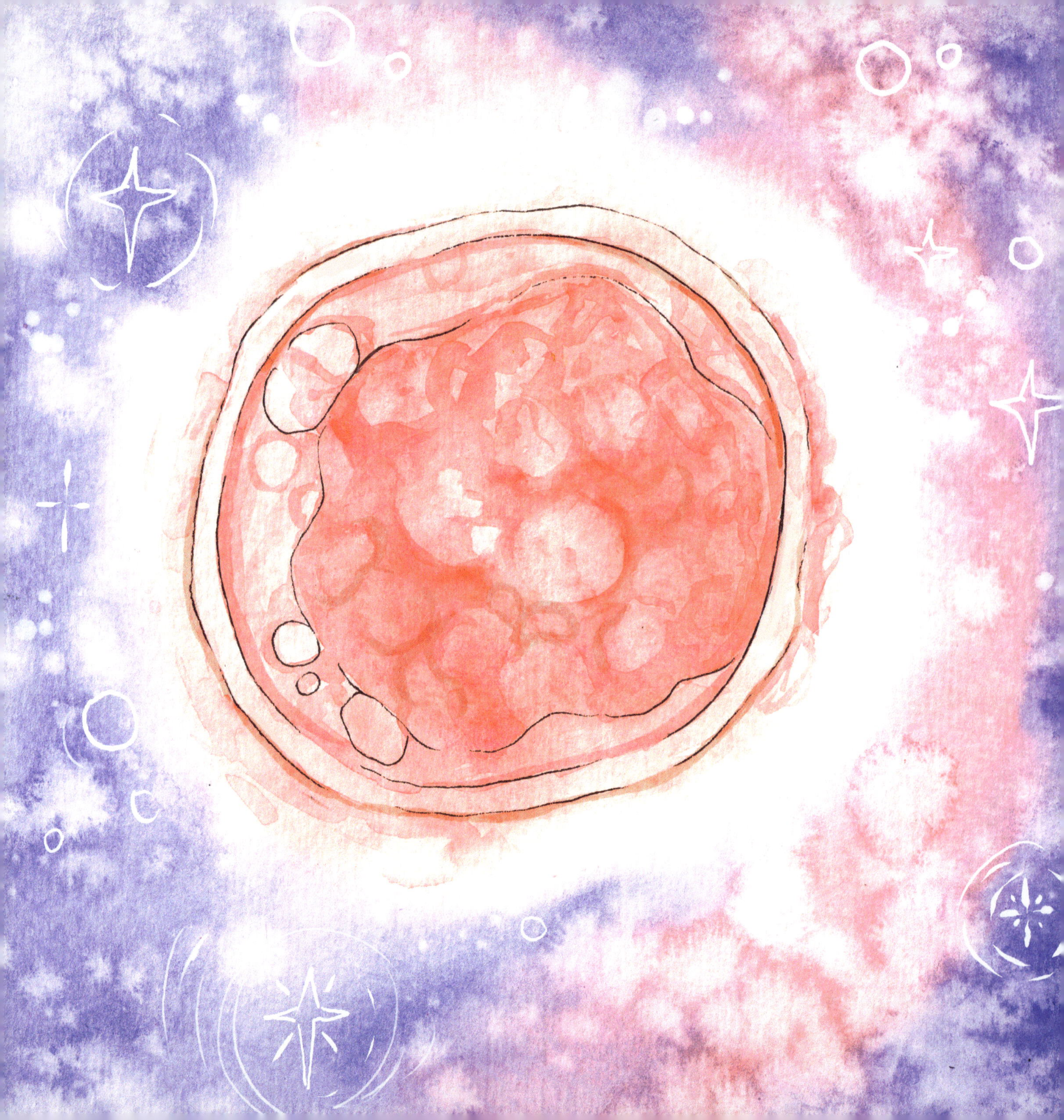

Set up warm and snug,
you could grow and bloom.
Now called "blast," prepared
to journey to the womb.

Down the tube you went,
a star on the display.
Arrived in your new home.
We hoped and wished you'd stay.

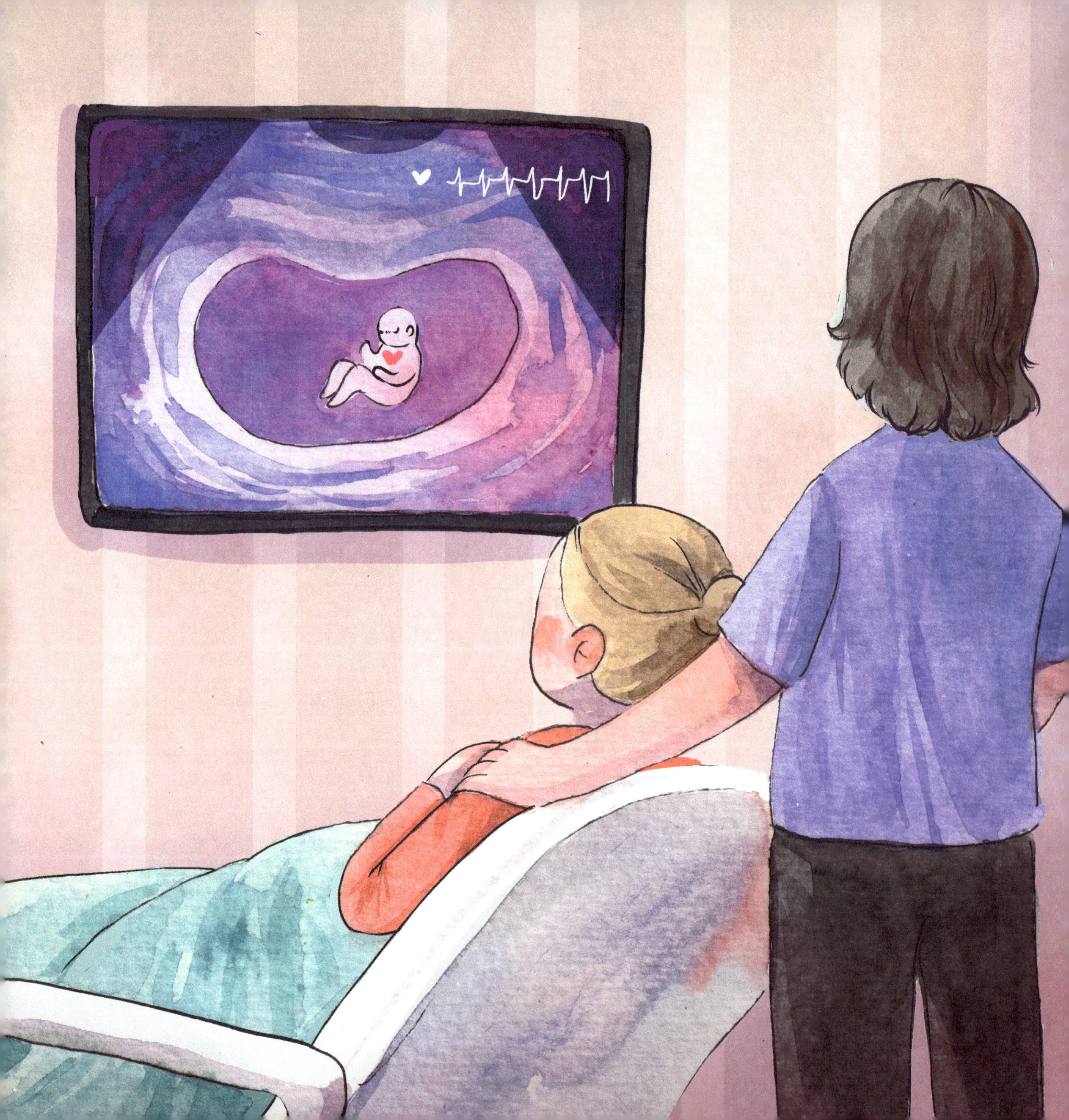

At last, the ultrasound.
We searched the tiny screen.
Your heartbeat flickered there.
We beamed that it was seen.

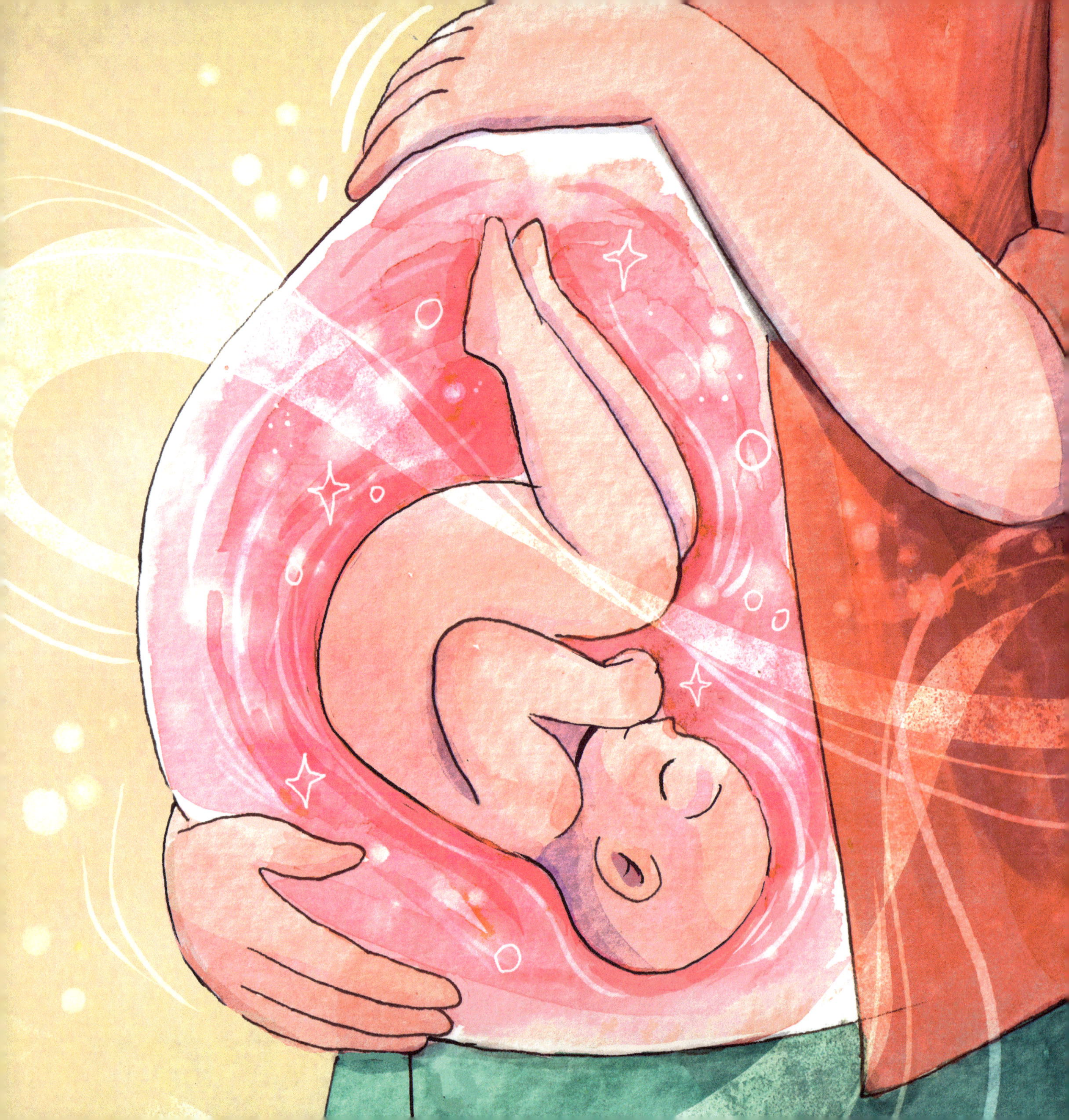

The wait seemed oh so long.
Nine months slowly passed.
On your birthday, though,
everything moved fast.

You cried, and so did we.

You were our child to keep.

Soft cheeks, chubby toes -

we gazed at you, asleep.

Through tears and bittersweet,
a journey tough, it's true.
Now our hearts are bright.
IVF helped bring us you. ♥

About the Author

Suzanne Castner is a devoted mother and wife, living a busy life filled with love. As a mother of four wonderful children—two daughters conceived through IVF and two lovely sons—Suzanne has experienced the incredible journey of parenthood in many forms. In addition to her role as a mother, Suzanne has been dedicated to the field of medicine, working as a primary care PA for the past 11 years.

"I've Always Loved You - An IVF Story" is her debut book, born from a heartfelt desire to find a story that could explain her daughters' unique conception. Suzanne's passion for storytelling and her personal experiences have come together to create a touching narrative that celebrates the miracle of life and the boundless love of family.